Water Lilies

and
Other Stories

CONTENTS

Steck-Vaughn Company

A Subsidiary of National Education Corporation

Did You Ever . . .?

Did you ever think where spiders go
In the middle of the night?
They don't have nests, or even holes,
But they're always out of sight.

Have you ever felt a tiny touch
On your leg beneath the sheet?
Perhaps **that's** where spiders go –
Snuggled up against your feet!

Penny Hegarty

The Carpenter and the Robin

Once upon a time there was a lonely carpenter.
He lived by himself in his warm little house.
One wet winter's day he saw a little robin with
a broken wing hopping about on the lawn.
The wind was blowing hard and the little bird was
fluffing up his feathers, trying to keep warm.

A cat was watching the robin from under a bush.

"Poor robin," said the carpenter.
"He's cold and wet and that cat will catch him because he can't fly away."

So the carpenter picked up a broom and ran out into the garden.
He chased the cat away and carried the robin gently into his warm house.

5

"I'll make you a cage," he said to the robin.
"Then you'll be safe from the cat
while your wing heals."

So he got a hammer and some nails and
some wood. He nailed the pieces of wood together
and made a cage for the robin.

He hung the cage in his window.
All winter he fed the robin and cared for it,
until one day he saw that its wing was better.
The bird was so happy that it began to sing.
The carpenter listened. "How beautiful," he thought.

But then the robin stopped singing.
It put its head under its wing and
it looked very sad.

"I am used to being alone," sighed the carpenter.
"But you need to be free, little robin."
So he opened the cage door and the bird flew away.

The next spring while the carpenter was
hammering away at his workbench, all alone
as usual, he heard singing outside his window.
He looked out and there on the window ledge
he saw two robins.
In their beaks the robins had moss and twigs.

All day the carpenter watched the birds
and all day they flew in and out of the cage
that he had thrown in the bushes.

"Look at that!" said the carpenter. "My robin
has come home and he's building his own nest
in the cage."

Very soon the nest was finished.
The carpenter saw that the robin and his mate
had filled the nest with eggs as blue as the sky.
And very soon after that, he saw
four baby robins peeping out of the nest.

As the carpenter listened they sang their songs.
He watched as the babies grew up and
in their turn flew away.

But when the winter came, his robin stayed on.
And every winter afterwards he sang to the carpenter
through the cold and the wind and the rain.

The Jay's New Feathers

Once upon a time there was a little jay
who lived all alone in the woods.
He had no friends and all the other birds
left him alone.
None of them noticed him.
One day he heard a great cry,
"Here come the peacocks. Here come the peacocks.
Make way! Make way!"
All the birds flew down to see
what the noise was about.
The jay wanted to see, too.
He hopped down onto a twig and
peeped around the tree.

He saw the peacocks walk proudly past.
   "We are the Kings of the Birds," they said and
opened their tails wide.
Their long tails opened like fans and
the colors glowed in the sun,
green and blue and gold.
   "Look at those fine tail feathers,"
said the jay. "That's why all the other birds
notice them.
I wish I had tail feathers like that.
Then the other birds would notice me, too."

As he hopped down the path, he saw
a long feather lying under a bush.
   "I'll have one fine feather at least,"
said the jay and put the feather in his beak.
Then he hopped a bit further along the path
and he found another feather.
Then he found another and another, until
his beak was quite full of feathers.

Then he had an idea.
He hid behind a bush and carefully stuck
the peacock feathers all over his body —
on his head and on his wings and on his tail.

"Now the other birds will think I am a peacock,"
he said. "Then they will notice me, too."

He hopped onto the path, and called
in a loud voice, "Make way! Make way!
Here comes the King of the Birds!"

All the birds flew down to see the peacock,
but – oh dear!
Just then the jay tripped on the long
tail feathers. He fell flat on his back.

All the other birds laughed.

"That's not a peacock," they said. "That's only
a silly jay pretending to be a peacock.
That's the King of the Clowns,
not the King of the Birds," and
they all roared with laughter.

The jay got up, feathers flapping over his eyes.
He wanted to fly away, but
all those feathers weighted him down.
He tried to run, but he couldn't see
where he was going.
Then he bumped right into the Chief Peacock,
who was standing in the path.

"Give me back our feathers,"
said the Chief Peacock. "No one can wear
our feathers," and he pulled them off the poor jay.

The jay hung his head. "I'm sorry," he said,
and flew off quickly into the trees.

He flew as far as he could,
until he was very tired.
Then he hopped onto a twig and looked around.
He was in a part of the woods
he had never been in before.

19

Then to his surprise, he heard a voice.

"What lovely blue feathers! What a fine color," said the voice.

The jay turned around and saw many other birds just like himself! The jay looked down at his own feathers and saw for the first time that they were a bright blue, even bluer than the other birds!

"Please stay with us," said the other jays.

"I will, I will," said the jay.

And so he did.

Water Lilies

A long time ago when the world was new people lived at peace with one another.
Everyone was happy in those days.
The fields were bright with flowers.
The forests were thick with trees.
Every tree and bush gave fruit.
The birds sang sweetly in the blue sky and the animals were not afraid.

Everyone had food in those days.
The people found everything they needed in
the fields and forests.
Then, at night, they sat outside their tepees and
told stories to one another.
Bright stars shone down on their bright new world.
The people sat at peace and watched the stars
move across the sky.

One night they saw a star brighter than
any other star.
It shone with a soft golden light.
As the people watched, it grew brighter.
"Look!" they said. "The star is coming nearer.
It is coming down to earth."
All at once, the star dropped down from the sky.
It hung like a golden bird above the mountain.

Night after night the people watched the star.
"What is the star doing?" they asked.
"Why has it come down to earth?
Why does it stay above the mountain?"
At last ten young braves went off to find
the star. When they came back they said,
"The star is shining in the top of the trees on
the mountain. She saw us, but she did not speak
to us. She is waiting for something."

One morning a young brave said,
"Last night I had a dream. A beautiful girl,
as bright as a star, stood by my side.
She shone with a soft golden light.
She called my name. She spoke to me.
But when I woke up, she was gone.
There was only the bright star above the mountain."

"What does she want?" asked the older men.

"She wants to live in our bright new world,"
said the brave.

"She is tired of moving across the sky.
She loves the fields and the forests.
She loves our birds and flowers.
She loves our people and our happy children.
She wants to make her home with us.
But she is afraid," said the brave.

"She is afraid our people will not love her."

The old men of the tribe held a powwow.
"The star wants to make her home with us,"
they said. "Our people are glad.
Let her come and live in our bright new world.
She can live in the top of a pine tree.
She can live in the heart of a flower.
Our people will love her."
They smoked their pipes of peace and
blew the warm smoke right up to the star.

Five young braves went out to meet her.
When they came back, a beautiful girl
floated softly behind them.
She filled the village
with a soft golden light.
   When the sun rose, she floated into the forest.
She floated to the top of a pine tree.
   "I will make my home here," she said.
   But after a day or two, she grew lonely.
No children came to the forest.
So she moved into the fields.

She made her home in the heart of a flower.
But there were big buffalo in the fields.
A great herd of buffalo ran by, **thud . . . thud . . .**
The star was afraid and could not rest.
She rose from the fields and floated on the wind.

"Poor star," said the people. "She cannot find
a home. Do not leave us, dear star.
Do not go back into the sky," they called.

  As the sun set, the star looked down
at the people she loved.
She floated above a lake.
In the water the sky looked black with
millions of tiny stars
and one very bright one.

  "Sisters! Sisters! Come down with me,"
she called. "Come and live in the land
of the happy children."

In the morning the people were glad.
Hundreds of beautiful white water lilies
floated on the lake.
The lilies were as bright as stars and
the heart of each one shone
with a soft, golden light.

Did You Ever . . .?

Did you ever stop to wonder why
The clouds don't tumble down?
How does the moon stay in the sky
And sail above the town?
I've tried to make my ball stay high
But always it comes down!
Why don't the stars fall from the sky
And twinkle on the ground?

Penny Hegarty